I0845725

JONATHA BLEZARD

MIDNIGHT IN PARIS

Parisian Dreams Unfold
Underneath the Moonlit Sky

At midnight, the city sometimes reveals its true essence, chaotic and beautiful at the same time. These two facets coexist harmoniously, offering a unique spectacle at every street corner. Some may be disappointed by the contrasting reality of the city, while others are pleasantly surprised by its diversity and vitality, which can sometimes be very harsh and aggressive. As a resident of Paris, I share with you my point of view, somewhat abstract and organic. No specific goal, other than observing people and fully experiencing the present moment. Let's walk together through the bustling streets of Paris, letting our senses guide us towards the unusual and the wonderful. Here, every encounter, every experience is an adventure in itself.

AU PIED DE COCHON
Les Halles

At midnight in Paris, life is still bustling in the bistros, with some staying open all night long. The chefs enter into a trance, shouting orders to their devoted staff who tirelessly fulfill their sacred mission despite the numerous burns and cuts. Paris is hungry, Paris is voracious and eats all the time, which is why it's a sacred and vital activity. It pulls into its neurosis a rich and thriving culinary scene. Chefs, in order to continue to exist, create, produce, and innovate relentlessly, knowing that a mistake and its repercussions can be fatal. Criticism is harsh, and clients are never fully satisfied.

LE LOUVRE

Le jardin des Tuileries

In the intense calm near the grand fountain, two friends sit beneath the attentive gaze of the stars and the moon, sharing with them their conversations, their voices hushing as they exchange intimate and sometimes very delicate and sensitive stories. With a backdrop of ancient statues and imposing columns that pretend not to understand what they're saying.

LA GARE DU NORD

18ᵉ arrondissement

The bustling hub of Paris's railway network, the last train departs, carrying with it the dreams and aspirations of travelers bound for destinations near and far. It's not always the warmest welcome one finds upon arriving in Paris. It's a station where the pulse of the city meets the rhythms of global travel, where fleeting encounters and grand farewells intersect under the flickering glow of departure boards. In the fading twilight, amidst the echoes of departing footsteps, the station stands as a monument to the transient nature of journeys, both physical and emotional. And yet, in its hustle and bustle, the Gare du Nord remains a symbol of possibility, where every departure signals the potential for new beginnings and untold adventures.

LE PIANISTE
Boulevard Richard-Lenoir

In the unassuming and dimly lit atmosphere of a small Parisian apartment, likely no larger than a pocket hand-kerchief, a classical pianist sits at the grand piano. Midnight might be the suitable hour to play, knowing that his neighbors have gone out and their newborn is staying with the grandmother, and the other neighbors next door have finally decided to turn off the television. He will surely play and enjoy a brief moment of happiness and fulfillment, but in at least 10 minutes, someone will come knocking on his door to ask him to stop playing. Midnight for a pianist in a Haussmannian apartment in Paris is indeed very rare to be heard in the end.

FILM SHOOTING
The Boulevard Périphérique

The renowned French film crew, a second world, a parallel universe, a beehive. They create, baptize, destroy, and rebuild. Filming the past as well as the future, cinema is part of Paris. But behind the spotlights and the cardboard sets lies a reality often dark and sad, a city where misery reigns in the most forgotten corners, far from the gazes captivated by the screens. While the cameras record the romanticized stories of the cobblestone streets and majestic buildings, the real inhabitants of Paris struggle for survival, forgotten and ignored. Sometimes, cinema only perpetuates an illusory dream, a huge contrast between the glamorous portrayal of the city and its true essence, where light does not erase the shadows of poverty and desolation.

CHEZ JEANNETTE

10ᵉ arrondissement

Towards midnight, everyone gathers here, people
from everywhere and all over the world, passing
through on missions or in search of inspiration, all
accompanied by a drink. And then, around midnight,
everyone, with a bit of inhibition, starts talking, talking a lot, even in the bars; everyone seems to know
better than others about the future, the present, and
the past. Everyone will try to assert their viewpoint,
and sometimes it ends in laughter, and sometimes in
a little argument, as we like to have here because in
Paris, we like to have the last word, and above all, not
to be wrong. But we do make encounters, for sure, and
sometimes some that change life from one day to the
next. You just have to look and not go back home too
early to sleep; you have to be patient and appreciate
the present moment.

LA SEINE

Île saint-louis

We see it passing in the distance, that little boat;
they seem to belong to another world. Everything
seems more beautiful over there. Everything is sus-
pended and calm, like on a postcard. Some even pass
by at full speed without anything stopping them; ama-
zed and surprised, we even wave at them from afar.
But it's usually just the tour boats that don't respond.
Sometimes we contemplate the Seine for hours, a bit
like staring into a fire, and on sunny days, we try to get
as close as possible to it to feel like we're at the sea-
side or to cool off. At midnight, we find ourselves in
solitude, sometimes finding comfort and serenity, or
simply calm. The Seine is beautiful nonetheless; it's a
shame we don't swim in it.

LA TOUR EIFFEL

7ᵉ arrondissement

It shines all night long, it never stops turning like a lighthouse, everyone must admire it. A powerful and international symbol, Paris, the City of Light, sometimes makes us forget reality. It enraptures us, especially for those who do not come from here. It's a bit of a symbol of a distant or out-of-step past. This massive metal tower tries to remind us of what Paris used to be, but it can't erase everything. It's a beautiful symbol, adding something for those who don't have much to think about and bringing a little light into the routine for some. But when the light turns and disappears, we find ourselves quite alone waiting for it to return. Under its glow, the dark streets come to life.

MAISON DE COUTURE
Rue Royale

In the workshops of grand fashion houses, it is sometimes at night that the magic happens, hidden behind thick curtains, even in places one wouldn't think of. These sublime and delicate artisans perform the most intricate operations in their beautiful white attire, in a state of trance where there is no room for hesitation. At midnight, their minds are of steel, and at this hour, everything is yet to be done; a long series of challenges begins for them. This part that is not suspected, these magnificent results require an extraordinary devotion and magic.

LE CAFÉ DU COIN

Montmartre

Some come every evening alone, to have a drink,
then two, then twelve of wine or anything that stings
and feels good. A bit disheveled and haggard, one might sometimes wait a long time for the idea, the stroke
of genius. Unfortunately, some never find it, but they
do find their way to the corner bar, yes. Some stay until
closing time, lost in the deepest thoughts. They keep
their eyes open to appear even more absent.
Don't bother asking them the time.

BASILIQUE DU SACRÉ-CŒUR

Montmartre

Tourists move in groups, sometimes in colonies, slowly led by a colorful umbrella, sometimes even a flag. Like a massive mass moving slowly. They cluster around a place like tentacles, taking photos behind their opaque glasses. We can't see their eyes.

We hear strange sounds and try to guess the origin. Their routes are very precise and organized, with each hour defined. There is a «them» and an «us» when we encounter them at the sites. Around midnight some-times, we see some intrepid ones leaving their group at night and venturing out as a couple or in small groups, finding them sitting on a terrace, then ending up laughing at the foot of the Sacré-Cœur. Happy with nothing, we envy them a little. The night will be long for them.

LE LOUVRE
La cour Marly

Here he is, alone, this guardian weary of the daily grind in the night. Sometimes a bit bitter about his situation. He may not see the end of his shift tonight, but he brought along a pastry; that will do. This man, alone, the great defender of all these wonders. The sole and final barrier against any intrusion and theft. Yet he remains always surprised and captivated by the sight of the full moon. Suddenly, everything stops for him. The light takes over. He is no longer here. At any moment, someone could attempt to enter and appropriate one of the wonders without defense. Tomorrow, this museum will be filled with visitors from around the world.

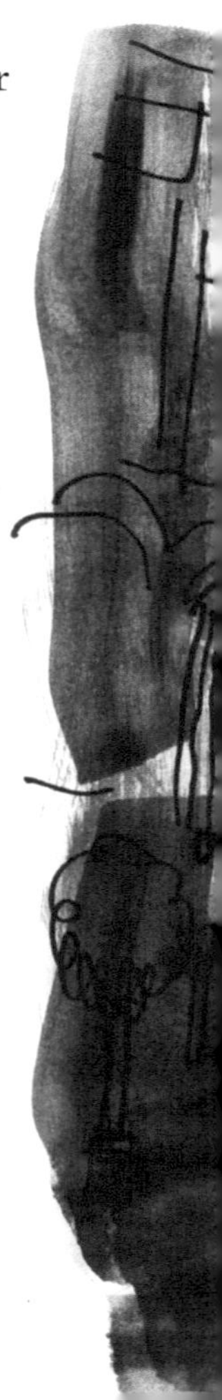

ARC DE TRIOMPHE

Place Charles-de-Gaulle

Here it is, tall, massive, and dominating everything that passes by, whoever it may be. The Arc de
Triomphe, an ancient relic reminding us of a distant
empire that once conquered such a vast kingdom that
we now try to appropriate it. Next to it, this sometimes brings us back to what we are and what can still
directly animate us in this city of madmen. What are
we doing here? Pedaling faster and faster in the endless
race. The city of Paris faster and even more always
more. Midnight slightly calms the traffic: at this hour,
we can sometimes, if we think about it, contemplate
the sky and the moon, and even better, breathe.

PLACE DES VOSGES

4ᵉ arrondissement

Sometimes, but it's very rare, you come across a night painter, and it's as if the world has stopped around him. But one wonders today if it's a happening performance or just a quest to find sleep, or simply someone who has lost his mind. For gone are those golden days when you'd come across painters in Paris working day and night on their canvases and finding the magic moment in the perfect light, our olds friends the Impressionists..

LE PONT NEUF

1ᵉ arrondissement

On the banks of the Seine, a group of dancers performs under the streetlights, their fluid and graceful movements swaying to the rhythm of the night. This is Paris, without inhibition or reservation, where we can dance wherever and however we please. They are there, with the ancient bridges and majestic monuments as a backdrop. In Paris, the night can be lively; sometimes the spectacle can be pleasant and surprising, but it's not always the case. «C'est la vie», as they say here. We zigzag between roses and rats, chaos and harmony come together and live side by side in a long, endless dance. It's always better to look towards the light.

PAINTER'S STUDIO
11ᵉ arrondissement

In his studio, he searches still and always, it's midnight and perhaps the moment when something pretends to want to see life. A spot, a sketch, a draft - everything appears. He loses himself in the creative process, every brushstroke bearing witness to his passion for his craft. This man can spend entire nights like this, seeking a piece of life hidden deep within himself. Inspiration is never far; it's woven into the very fabric of the city, waiting to be discovered by those who have the vision to see it at midnight in Paris.

On the rooftop terrace of a Haussmann-style building, a couple lounges, the warmth enveloping them, needing little more to be content. For a brief moment, they sail above all their problems, seeing everything with a touch of lightness. Their hearts filled with the promise of a new beginning. Against the backdrop of the moonlit sky, they become a testament to the enduring power of love..

DANSE POPULAIRE
Utopie

In the shadowy recesses of an ancient square, a lone dancer spins gracefully in the moonlight, her movements fluid and effortless as she loses herself in the music. Against the backdrop of centuries-old buildings and cobblestone streets, she becomes a living embodiment of Parisian elegance and charm, her passion for dance evident in every step and gesture.

In the quiet hours of the night, the city becomes her stage, as she twirls and leaps with abandon, her spirit soaring on the gentle breeze that rustles through the trees. In Paris, the night is alive with the sound of applause and admiration, as spectators from around the world come together to share in the magic of the city of lights.

LE BOULANGER

Utopie

At dawn, a baker kneads the dough with practiced hands, the smell of freshly baked bread filling the air as he prepares for the day ahead. He is a symbol of tradition and craftsmanship, his dedication to his craft evident in every perfectly formed loaf and every flaky croissant. In Paris, the art of baking is more than just a profession; it is a way of life. People line up regardless of the weather and inconvenience. And even more than that, they respect the queue; it's a moment of respite while outside of this context, Parisians live fast and without a minute to spare, as if their lives depended on it every second.

LE MÉTRO

Ligne 4

And here we are in the last metro crossing the city,
a metro often bustling. We find ourselves there, dazed
and pensive. The lights blind us. In the metro, we're
all in the same boat, in these heavy and noisy carriages
with strong and harsh odors. One last metro before
Paris settles into a peaceful sleep, its streets empty ex-
cept for the secrets whispered by lovers and dreamers.
With the silhouette of the city and the twinkling stars
in the background, it becomes a canvas for the imagi-
nation, while dreams soar on the gentle breeze rustling
through the trees

Cover Design, Illustrations, Graphic Design, and Layout by Jonathan Blezard

The cover and all illustrations in this coloring book were created by Jonathan Blezard. Additionally, the graphic design and layout of this book were meticulously crafted by the same artist.

Published by Mélot du Dy, Jonathan Blezard represents **Mélot du Dy** in the creation and publication of this work. For permissions, rights, and inquiries, please contact: **blezardjonathan1@gmail.com**

Mélot du Dy publishing, Thank you for supporting the arts and independent publishing

Lebanon / France 2024